"We conclude that in the field of public education, the doctrine of 'separate but equal' has no place."

—Chief Justice Earl Warren,

Brown v. Board of Education

(May 17, 1954)

BROWN V. BOARD OF EDUCATION: THE BATTLE FOR EQUAL EDUCATION

BY BARBARA A. SOMERVILL

Content Adviser: Joanna Banks,
Museum Educator, Washington, D.C.

Published in the United States of America by The Child's World®
PO Box 326
Chanhassen, MN 55317-0326
800-599-READ
www.childsworld.com

The Child's World®: Mary Berendes, Publishing Director
Editorial Directions, Inc.: E. Russell Primm, Editorial Director; Emily J. Dolbear,
Line Editor; Katie Marsico, Assistant Editor; Matthew Messbarger, Editorial Assistant;
Susan Hindman, Copy Editor; Sarah E. De Capua, Proofreader; Marsha Bonnoit,
Peter Garnham, Terry Johnson, Chris Simms, and Stephan Carl Wender,
Fact Checkers; Tim Griffin/IndexServ, Indexer; Dawn Friedman,
Photo Researcher; Linda S. Koutris, Photo Selector

The Child's World® and Journey to Freedom® are the sole property
and registered trademarks of The Child's World®

Cover photograph: Linda Brown, front center, in her classroom at Monroe School in 1953
© Carl Iwasaki/Time Life Pictures/Getty Images

Interior photographs © Courtesy of the NAACP/AP/Wide World Photos: 19;
AP/Wide World Photos: 22; Bettmann/Corbis: 9, 11, 13, 15, 16, 21, 24, 26, 27, 31;
Corbis: 10; Jack Moebes/Corbis: 30; David Butow/Corbis SABA: 32; Will & Deni
McIntyre/Corbis: 36; Carl Iwasaki/Time Life Pictures/Getty Images: 2, 6, 8;
Hulton|Archive/Getty Images: 14, 28; Hank Walker/Time Life Pictures/Getty
Images: 17; Ed Clark/Time Life Pictures/Getty Images: 23; Margaret Bourke-White/
Time Life Pictures/Getty Images: 25; Grey Villet/Time Life Pictures/Getty Images: 29;
Don Hogan Charles/New York Times Co./Getty Images: 35; Al Ravenna/New York
World-Telegram and the Sun Newspaper Photograph Collection/Library of Congress: 20.

Library of Congress Cataloging-in-Publication Data
Somervill, Barbara A.
Brown v. Board of Education : the battle for equal education / by Barbara A. Somervill.
v. cm. — (Journey to freedom)
Includes bibliographical references.
Contents: A long walk to school — Separate ... not equal — Brown v.
Board of Education—Desegregation—Linda Brown's legacy—Timeline.
ISBN 1-59296-229-7 (Library bound : alk. paper) 1. Segregation in education—Law and legislation—
United States—Juvenile literature. 2. Discrimination in education—Law and legislation—United States—
Juvenile literature. 3. Brown, Oliver, 1918– —Trials, litigation, etc.—Juvenile literature. 4. Topeka (Kan.).
Board of Education—Trials, litigation, etc.—Juvenile literature. [1. Segregation in education—Law and
legislation. 2. African Americans—Civil rights. 3. Brown, Oliver, 1918– —Trials, litigation, etc.] I. Title:
Brown versus Board of Education. II. Title. III. Series.
KF4155.Z9S63 2004
344.73'0798—dc22   2003027079

Contents

LINDA BROWN STANDS IN FRONT OF TOPEKA'S SEGREGATED MONROE ELEMENTARY SCHOOL IN 1953.

A Long Walk to School

It was an ordinary school day in Topeka, Kansas, in 1950. Linda Brown was in the third grade at Monroe Elementary School. To get to school, Linda had to walk six blocks, cross railroad tracks, and wait for a bus.

On this day, her father would walk her to the bus stop. Linda picked up her books and her lunch. Reverend Oliver Brown and his daughter headed down the street. Six blocks from their home, they passed Sumner Elementary School. Brown entered the school and requested to see the principal. Then he asked if his daughter could enroll at Sumner because it was so much closer to home.

The principal of Sumner refused Brown's request. Sumner was an all-white school, and Linda Brown was African-American. Schools in Kansas in the 1950s were **segregated** by race. Separating African-American children from white children in this way was perfectly legal. In 1896, the Supreme Court had ruled that states could provide "separate but equal" facilities for blacks and whites. *Equal* may have sounded fair, but linked with the word *separate,* it usually meant much lower quality for blacks than whites.

Brown decided he wanted to sue the group that ran the school system—the board of education—in Topeka. But he needed help. He got that help from other African-American parents in Topeka and from the country's largest and oldest civil rights organization, the National Association for the Advancement of Colored People (NAACP).

Brown spoke with other African-American parents about the unfairness of segregated schools. With legal help from the NAACP, the parents joined together and filed a **lawsuit** that came to be known as *Brown v. Board of Education*. NAACP lawyers presented the case in the U.S. **District Court** of Kansas. When the case failed, they **appealed** the decision to the U.S. Supreme Court.

It took three years before the Supreme Court delivered a final decision on *Brown v. Board of Education*. Its decision changed life in the United States forever.

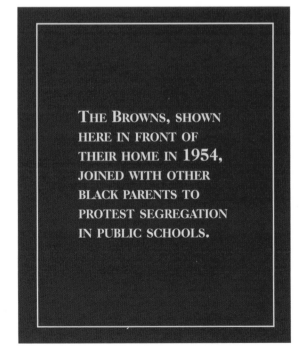

THE BROWNS, SHOWN HERE IN FRONT OF THEIR HOME IN **1954**, JOINED WITH OTHER BLACK PARENTS TO PROTEST SEGREGATION IN PUBLIC SCHOOLS.

Separate . . . Not Equal

The end of the Civil War should have provided great opportunity for blacks in the United States. In 1868, African-Americans became free citizens with full rights under the 14th Amendment to the U.S. Constitution. That is what the law said, but the reality for blacks in the South was quite different. Power, money, and land in the South remained in the hands of whites who did not want blacks to be equal under the law.

By the 1870s, state governments in the South passed many laws to restrict the rights of blacks. They were called Jim Crow laws, after a character in a popular song from the 1800s that made fun of African-Americans. The song might have made some people laugh, but the laws were not funny. They took rights away from citizens.

THE 14TH AMENDMENT HAD LITTLE EFFECT ON FREED SLAVES LIKE THESE PEANUT PICKERS IN VIRGINIA.

I n the late 1800s, a Louisiana law required separate train facilities for blacks and whites. African-Americans rode in railroad cars labeled "colored" with hard wooden seats and little fresh air. The cars often rode directly behind coal cars, so travelers also had to breathe coal dust. In 1892, an African-American named Homer Plessy was put in jail for sitting in the whites-only car of the East Louisiana Railroad. He filed a lawsuit to challenge Louisiana's Jim Crow law.

Plessy v. Ferguson, as the case was called, claimed that separate train facilities violated the 14th Amendment. The case was unsuccessful in the U.S. District Court of Louisiana. In 1896, *Plessy v. Ferguson* went to the U.S. Supreme Court. The Court ruled that if the facilities were "separate but equal," no rights were violated. The Court's ruling ended any chance for African-Americans to be treated truly as equals.

The South took the Court at its word. African-Americans throughout the South used separate water fountains, rest rooms, and restaurants. They sat in the rear of buses or in railroad cars marked "colored." They went to all-black theaters, shops, and schools. Everything, said southern white lawmakers, was "separate but equal."

But there was little equality when it came to education. In 1948, for blacks in South Carolina's Clarendon County, the school term never lasted longer than six months. No school was held during planting and harvest seasons, when many black children worked in the fields. Classes were huge, with sometimes 50 or more children to one teacher. The schools themselves were little more than ramshackle cabins, often with no running water. Students used outhouses instead of indoor toilets. There was no heat in the winter, and the roofs leaked. Students sat at rickety tables and used out-of-date textbooks.

For white children in Clarendon County, school was held in buildings with heat, water, and rest rooms. Students attended a full school year. They studied from new books and sat at comfortable desks. Classes had only 20 to 25 students.

Despite these differences, Clarendon County officials claimed both school systems were "equal." The county's board of education spent $43 a year on each African-American student and $180 on each white student. This kind of difference existed in many parts of the country. For example, that same year, public schools in Atlanta, Georgia, spent $228 on each black student and $570 on each white student.

The Clarendon County educational system was typical of segregated schooling. No white teachers taught at all-black schools. No African-American teachers stepped foot in all-white schools. Some black teachers had college degrees, but others barely had a fourth-grade education. In addition, school districts did not plan on black students wanting a higher education. Sunflower County, Mississippi, for example, had no high school for African-Americans.

IN THE 1940s, BLACK SCHOOLS WERE OFTEN INFERIOR TO WHITE SCHOOLS. THIS SCHOOL FOR AFRICAN-AMERICANS IN GEORGIA HAD ONE TEACHER.

The segregated educational system created a cycle of poverty and ignorance. Without education, blacks had to work as maids, laborers, and farmworkers.

African-Americans wanted better lives for their children. They understood that a high-quality education would improve their lives. Some of those people fought for greater educational opportunities. Some even won their battles.

Mae Bertha Carter, the daughter of **sharecroppers,** grew up in the 1930s in Sunflower County, Mississippi. She worked the cotton fields in spring, summer, and fall and went to school for only three months a year. She left school at the age of 10, barely able to read and write. But as a parent in the 1960s, Carter was determined that her children would get out of the fields. She worked tirelessly for educational change in her local school system. Her youngest eight children were able to attend—and graduate from—**integrated** schools in Mississippi.

George McLaurin also wanted more in life. In 1938, the Supreme Court had ruled that states providing graduate programs for whites had to offer "separate but equal" programs for blacks. McLaurin was accepted at the University of Oklahoma's graduate school of education in 1948. As a segregated student, he attended class by himself or sat at a desk roped off from other students, ate in a separate section of the cafeteria, and studied in a separate part of the library. McLaurin decided to file suit against the University of Oklahoma, challenging the school's "separate but equal" policy.

AS A BLACK STUDENT AT THE UNIVERSITY OF OKLAHOMA'S GRADUATE SCHOOL OF EDUCATION, GEORGE McLAURIN WAS FORCED TO SIT SEPARATELY FROM THE WHITE STUDENTS. HE DECIDED TO SUE THE UNIVERSITY IN 1948.

McLaurin's **attorney** in the case was the NAACP's chief lawyer, Thurgood Marshall, who in 1967 became the first African-American to serve on the Supreme Court. As an attorney, Marshall argued in court that the University of Oklahoma treated George McLaurin as a lesser person. In 1950, the Supreme Court ruled in McLaurin's favor, and the University of Oklahoma was forced to end its segregated policies.

In a less successful case, South Carolinian Levi Pearson sued his local school board in 1947 to get school busing for his children. Since the district provided buses for whites, he claimed, it should do the same for African-Americans. Local whites blocked Pearson's efforts. He lost credit at stores and local banks. He could not buy farm supplies or sell his crops. He watched his crops wither in the fields. And he lost his lawsuit.

SCHOOL DISTRICTS IN THE SOUTH PROVIDED BUS SERVICE FOR WHITE STUDENTS ONLY.

It was clear that black parents needed help to get an equal education for their children. During the early 1950s, the NAACP provided these parents with legal strategies and lawyers.

The lawsuits they filed challenged *Plessy v. Ferguson*'s "separate but equal" ruling. These lawsuits forced the issue of equal education onto the **docket** of the highest court in the country.

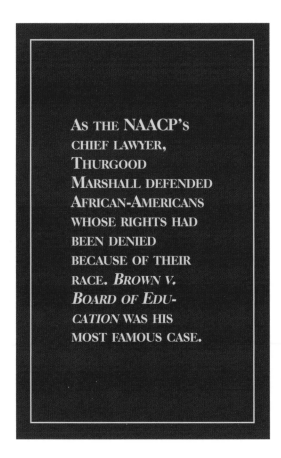

AS THE NAACP'S CHIEF LAWYER, THURGOOD MARSHALL DEFENDED AFRICAN-AMERICANS WHOSE RIGHTS HAD BEEN DENIED BECAUSE OF THEIR RACE. *BROWN V. BOARD OF EDUCATION* WAS HIS MOST FAMOUS CASE.

Brown v. Board of Education

I t was in this climate of unrest that the U.S. District Court of Kansas first heard the Brown case in June 1951. The lawyers for the Topeka Board of Education argued that Linda Brown received a "separate but equal" education. They claimed that she had a school, teachers, and the same **curriculum** as white children in Topeka, Kansas. The district court agreed. The NAACP lawyers appealed the district court decision all the way to the U.S. Supreme Court.

At about the same time, several other lawsuits dealing with "separate but equal" education failed. They were also appealed to the Supreme Court. These cases included *Briggs v. Elliot* in South Carolina; *Davis v. School Board of Prince Edward County, Virginia;* and *Belton v. Gebhart* in Delaware.

The *Briggs v. Elliot* case represented 20 parents in Clarendon County, South Carolina. Harry Briggs was first in the alphabetical listing of parents. R. W. Elliot served as president of the county school board. The case asked the county to provide school bus service for African-American students. The court's first ruling ordered the school board to make the schools equal. The decision did not require ending segregated schools in Clarendon County.

Davis v. School Board of Prince Edward County, Virginia represented 117 African-American students from Moton High School, including a ninth grader named Dorothy E. Davis. The all-black school was run-down and overcrowded. Some students attended class in tar-paper shacks. The students protested, and NAACP lawyers sued in their names.

NAACP LAWYERS, LED BY THURGOOD MARSHALL (SECOND FROM RIGHT), MOUNTED A LEGAL ATTACK AGAINST SCHOOL SEGREGATION. *BROWN V. BOARD OF EDUCATION* WENT BEFORE THE U.S. SUPREME COURT IN 1954.

The last case, *Belton v. Gebhart,* pitted Ethel Belton and other African-Americans against Francis Gebhart, a member of the Claymont Board of Education in Delaware. This case claimed that Delaware provided black children with a lesser education than white children.

These three cases were similar to *Brown v. Board of Education.* Each of the decisions stated that the children received a "separate but equal" education. So when the cases reached the Supreme Court, they were grouped together under the title *Brown v. Board of Education.*

THE WORK OF KENNETH CLARK, SPEAKING HERE TO THE U.S. SENATE ABOUT EQUAL EDUCATION IN 1970, SHOWED THAT SEGREGATION DAMAGED THE SELF-ESTEEM OF BLACK STUDENTS.

In court before the Supreme Court justices, the NAACP lawyers presented information about the damaging emotional effect of segregated schools on African-American children. Dr. Kenneth Clark, a black professor at City College of New York, tested children using two dolls. Most of the children were African-American. The dolls were exactly alike except for their skin color. One doll was white; the other had brown skin.

Clark asked each child several questions. He asked which was the "bad" doll and which was the "good" doll. He asked which doll the child most wanted to play with. Then, he asked which doll looked most like the child being tested. Most children said the brown-skinned doll was "bad" and the white doll was "good." Clark showed that black children had developed a poor view of themselves and their race. He said segregated schools were partly to blame.

As in the McLaurin trial, the main lawyer for the people filing the lawsuits was Thurgood Marshall. Marshall argued that money and schools were not the worst problems with "separate but equal" education. He said African-American children suffered because segregation existed.

The Supreme Court agreed. On May 17, 1954, Chief Justice Earl Warren read the Court's decision: "In the field of public education, the doctrine of 'separate but equal' has no place. Separate educational facilities are . . . unequal." Marshall was thrilled. He said later, "I was so happy I was numb."

ON THE STEPS OF THE U.S. SUPREME COURT BUILDING, THURGOOD MARSHALL CELEBRATES WITH OTHER NAACP LAWYERS AFTER THE COURT RULED AGAINST SCHOOL SEGREGATION ON MAY 17, 1954.

Not everyone felt the same joy as Marshall. Many people in the southern states were angry that the Court had meddled in state business. So many people would resist change in their schools that **desegregation** would not begin immediately.

In Washington, D.C., Bryant Bowles founded the National Association for the Advancement of White People. He wanted to stop desegregation any way he could. Bowles asked whites to stop their children from attending mixed-race schools.

Clearly, desegregation would face many barriers. Governors and law-makers in the South were afraid to push school changes. Most southern voters were white. Politicians did not want to take an unpopular stand and support desegregation. As fall approached, the South prepared for protests, violence, and change.

BRYANT BOWLES, FOUNDER OF THE NATIONAL ASSOCIATION FOR THE ADVANCEMENT OF WHITE PEOPLE, SPEAKS AT A RALLY IN DELAWARE IN 1954.

Desegregation

Some schools accepted the *Brown v. Board of Education* decision. Baltimore, Maryland, officials, for example, were prepared for the ruling. In September 1954, the city's 189 schools were opened to African-American children. Angry whites protested outside a dozen schools. By October, tensions had risen and fights broke out in the streets.

WHITE HIGH SCHOOL STUDENTS PROTEST INTEGRATION IN BALTIMORE, MARYLAND.

In northeastern Virginia, most people accepted the change. African-Americans attended previously all-white schools with few problems. However, southern Virginia schools put up a fight. The state's governor, Thomas Stanley, declared, "I shall use every legal means at my command to continue segregated schools in Virginia."

Governor Stanley had plenty of company. Governors in many southern states opposed the law. They refused to desegregate public schools. North Carolina passed a law making local school boards responsible for desegregation. This law made fighting for desegregation more difficult. If school districts resisted the law, lawsuits had to be filed against each district.

In 1955, the Supreme Court added to its first decision on *Brown*. The Court said school desegregation should take place with "all deliberate speed." This decision, called *Brown II,* gave southern states greater opportunity to drag their feet. "All deliberate speed" did not name a specific date by which all schools had to follow the law. Slow-moving school boards claimed they were moving as fast as they could—at a snail's pace.

GOVERNOR THOMAS STANLEY OF VIRGINIA FOUGHT AGAINST DESEGREGATING HIS STATE'S PUBLIC SCHOOLS. STANLEY SERVED AS GOVERNOR OF VIRGINIA FROM 1954 TO 1958.

President Dwight Eisenhower was uneasy about the Supreme Court's decision in *Brown*. He knew desegregation would not be quick or easy. Eisenhower said, "The fellow who tries to tell me that you can do these things by force is just plain nuts." Eisenhower did not want to use his presidential power to change southern opinions. However, the situation in Little Rock, Arkansas, forced his hand.

In 1957, the governor of Arkansas, Orval Faubus, tested the Court's decision. He ordered the state's **National Guard** to prevent nine black students from entering Central High School in Little Rock.

One of those students, Elizabeth Eckford, later described her experience: "The crowd was quiet. I guess they were waiting to see what was going to happen. When I was able to steady my knees, I walked up to the guard who had let the white students in. He, too, didn't move. When I tried to squeeze past him, he raised his bayonet, and then the other guards closed in, and they raised their bayonets." The black students were pushed and prodded, and violence broke out.

President Eisenhower then ordered U.S. Army troops to Little Rock to keep the peace. Soldiers lined up on both sides of the black students and escorted them into the school. Central High now had an integrated student body.

IN 1957, U.S. SOLDIERS ESCORTED BLACK STUDENTS INTO CENTRAL HIGH SCHOOL IN LITTLE ROCK, ARKANSAS. PRESIDENT EISENHOWER HAD ORDERED THE TROOPS TO ENFORCE INTEGRATION AT THE SCHOOL.

The Central High event was one of many battles that blacks won. Each time a school district tried to prevent desegregation, supporters of *Brown v. Board of Education* stepped forward. The process was slow, and attempts to block desegregation arose at every level.

In 1961, a black student named James Meredith wanted to study at the University of Mississippi. As a Mississippi resident, he had the right to attend Ole Miss. But Ole Miss had remained all white. After the school rejected his application, Meredith filed a lawsuit against the university.

He lost his case in Mississippi but won on appeal to the Supreme Court. Yet, when Meredith tried to sign up for classes, university officials refused to admit him. Finally, President John F. Kennedy ordered Mississippi's National Guard to protect Meredith so he could register at the school. After protests during which two people were killed, Meredith began classes and later graduated from the university.

Students such as the nine African-Americans at Central High School and James Meredith opened the door for other blacks. Slowly, more public schools and state universities accepted African-American students. Finally, the opportunities promised at the end of the Civil War were becoming a reality.

IN 1958, ERNEST GREEN (CENTER) BECAME THE FIRST AFRICAN-AMERICAN TO GRADUATE FROM CENTRAL HIGH SCHOOL IN LITTLE ROCK, ARKANSAS.

By 1964, MOST PUBLIC SCHOOLS WERE DESEGREGATED IN THE UNITED STATES. AFRICAN-AMERICAN AND WHITE STUDENTS LEARNED IN THE SAME CLASSROOMS.

Linda Brown's Legacy

Many people consider *Brown v. Board of Education* the springboard to the civil rights movement. It was certainly a major victory, but the ruling did not offer as much change as some people hoped. It did not end segregation in the South. Black children who attended schools with white children were still banned from public parks. They still rode in the rear of the bus and drank from "colored only" water fountains.

By 1964, about 90 percent of southern schools had desegregated. That did not mean that all schools had a racial balance. Since children went to school near their homes, which were often in all-black neighborhoods, many schools had mostly black students.

AFTER THE *BROWN* RULING, IT WAS STILL LEGAL TO FORCE BLACKS IN THE SOUTH TO SIT AT THE BACK OF PUBLIC BUSES.

The solution to this problem in the 1970s was busing. In an attempt to create balanced schools, white students were bused to mostly black schools, and black students were bused to mostly white schools. Although busing did improve integration, it proved to be expensive and ineffective. And no one wanted children to have to travel great distances when a perfectly good school was just a few blocks away. The practice of busing to integrate schools eventually faded out, leaving children to attend neighborhood schools.

Equal education was also an issue at the college level. After high school, African-American students weren't going to college as often as white students. A policy called affirmative action was started to increase the numbers of minorities (and women) on campuses. Affirmative action gave African-Americans a boost in being admitted to colleges and universities. This policy was also meant to help minorities and women in the workplace.

Over the years, people have supported affirmative action for different reasons. They believe African-Americans as a group should benefit after suffering past **discrimination.** They might also believe affirmative action is necessary because discrimination still exists. Or they might like the idea of bringing students from different races together on college campuses. But many other people oppose affirmative action. They believe that individuals should be judged according to their abilities. They also believe it is unfair for students to receive any special treatment based on their race or sex.

AFFIRMATIVE ACTION CONTINUES TO BE A CONTROVERSIAL ISSUE IN THE UNITED STATES. THIS YOUNG GIRL SHOWS HER SUPPORT FOR AFFIRMATIVE ACTION AT A RALLY IN BERKELEY, CALIFORNIA, IN 1995.

In the 1990s, white students who believed they were victims of affirmative action began to file lawsuits. They said that they suffered because African-Americans were favored because of their race. In 2003, the Supreme Court decided that universities could consider race when admitting students. However, race could not be the main reason for acceptance.

As for Linda Brown, she never went to all-white Sumner School. She grew up and got married. Her own children attended segregated public schools in Topeka. It was not until 1994 that Topeka finally made a workable desegregation plan. At that time, Linda Brown Thompson said, "Sometimes I wonder if we really did the children and the nation a favor by taking this case to the Supreme Court. I know it was the right thing for my father and others to do then. But after nearly 40 years, we find the Court's ruling unfulfilled."

Linda Brown Thompson spoke her feelings truthfully. But it is also true that thousands of other African-Americans have graduated from southern high schools, colleges, and universities since 1954. They have used their educations to make invaluable contributions in every field. Many of those contributions would not have happened without *Brown v. Board of Education.*

LINDA BROWN THOMPSON, SHOWN HERE SPEAKING TO REPORTERS IN 1984, NEVER ATTENDED AN INTEGRATED SCHOOL. THOMPSON'S ROLE IN THE DESEGREGATION OF PUBLIC SCHOOLS IN THE UNITED STATES WAS HISTORIC.

Because of the *Brown* ruling, spending in public schools is now based on the number of students, regardless of race. Students of all backgrounds learn side by side and from each other. They take part in sports, the arts, and all other school activities together. *Brown v. Board of Education* may not have delivered immediate results, but this single lawsuit did bring about monumental change for the country's children. All Americans have gained from the equal education that African-Americans like Oliver Brown and Thurgood Marshall fought for decades ago.

THE WINNERS OF THE BATTLE FOR EQUAL EDUCATION ARE TODAY'S STUDENTS, WHO ATTEND CLASSES TOGETHER BECAUSE OF *BROWN V. BOARD OF EDUCATION.*

Timeline

1863	Abraham Lincoln, the 16th U.S. president, issues the Emancipation Proclamation.
1866	The 14th Amendment is proposed. It is approved in 27 of the 38 states in 1868.
1875	Congress passes the Civil Rights Act of 1875, which outlaws discrimination in hotels, theaters, and other public places.
1896	The Supreme Court decision *Plessy v. Ferguson* allows states to provide "separate but equal" facilities for African-Americans and whites.
1909	The National Association for the Advancement of Colored People (NAACP) is formed to lead the struggle for civil rights for African-Americans.
1938	The Supreme Court rules that states with graduate programs for whites have to offer "separate but equal" programs for blacks.
1947	African-American Levi Pearson sues his local school board in South Carolina to get school busing for his children. He loses the case.
1950	The Supreme Court rules that the University of Oklahoma must end its segregated policies.
1951	The *Brown v. Board of Education* lawsuit is filed in Topeka, Kansas.
1952	The Supreme Court hears arguments in the *Brown v. Board of Education* case.
1954	The Supreme Court outlaws segregation in public schools in its *Brown v. Board of Education* decision.
1955	In *Brown II,* the Supreme Court says that school desegregation should take place with "all deliberate speed." African-Americans in Montgomery, Alabama, start a boycott of the city's bus system because of segregated seating.
1956	The Supreme Court outlaws segregation on Alabama buses.
1957	Escorted by U.S. Army troops, nine African-American students integrate Central High School in Little Rock, Arkansas.
1962	James Meredith becomes the first African-American student at the University of Mississippi.
1964	President Lyndon Johnson signs the Civil Rights Act of 1964, making segregation in hotels, restaurants, stadiums, and other public places illegal. About 90 percent of southern schools are desegregated.
1965	President Johnson signs the Voting Rights Act, guaranteeing all U.S. citizens the right to vote.
1971	The Supreme Court rules in favor of busing students to desegregate public schools.
1994	Topeka finally makes a workable desegregation plan for its public schools.
2003	The Supreme Court rules that universities may consider race when admitting students, as long as it is not the main reason.

Glossary

appealed (uh-PEELD)
To appeal means to ask that a higher court or judge reconsider a court decision. NAACP lawyers appealed the *Brown v. Board of Education* decision to the U.S. Supreme Court.

attorney (uh-TUR-nee)
An attorney is a lawyer. In *Brown v. Board of Education* and several other civil rights cases, the attorney for the people who brought the lawsuits was Thurgood Marshall.

curriculum (kuh-RIK-yuh-luhm)
A curriculum is a school's program of study, such as reading, mathematics, and science. The Topeka Board of Education lawyers argued that Linda Brown received the same curriculum as white children in Topeka, Kansas.

desegregation (DEE-seh-greh-GAY-shun)
Desegregation is ending the practice of separating races in public facilities. Desegregation in public schools did not begin immediately after the *Brown* ruling.

discrimination (diss-KRIM-uh-NAY-shun)
Discrimination is the act of treating people unfairly based on their race, sex, or background. Supporters of affirmative action believe African-Americans as a group should benefit after suffering past discrimination.

district court (DISS-trikt KORT)
A district court is the first court to hear a case that deals with federal crime. The U.S. District Court of Kansas was the first to hear the arguments in *Brown v. Board of Education.*

docket (DOK-it)
A docket is a list of lawsuits to be tried by a court. The NAACP forced the issue of equal education onto the docket of the Supreme Court.

integrated (IN-teh-grayt-ed)
Integrated means all races are included. Today, most schools are racially integrated.

lawsuit (LAW-soot)
A lawsuit is a legal action or case brought against a person or group in a court of law. In 1951, Oliver Brown brought a lawsuit against the Topeka Board of Education.

National Guard (NASH-uh-nuhl GARD)
The National Guard is a U.S. military organization with units in each state. In 1957, Governor Orval Faubus ordered the state's National Guard to prevent black students from entering Central High School in Little Rock.

segregated (SEH-greh-gat-ed)
Segregated means kept separate, particularly in regard to race. From the late 1800s to the mid-1900s, laws in the South segregated blacks from whites.

sharecroppers (SHAIR-krop-purz)
Sharecroppers are workers who farm the land for the owner in return for part of the crops. Mae Bertha Carter, a civil rights activist, was the daughter of sharecroppers.

Index

Further Information

Books

Anderson, Wayne. *Brown v. Board of Education: The Case against School Segregation.* New York: Rosen Publishing, 2003.

Anderson, Wayne. *Plessy v. Ferguson: Legalizing Segregation.* New York: Rosen Publishing, 2003.

O'Neill, Laurie A. *Little Rock: The Desegregation of Central High.* Brookfield, Conn.: Millbrook Press, 1994.

Takach, James. *Brown v. Board of Education.* San Diego: Lucent Books, 1998.

Williams, Carla. *Thurgood Marshall.* Chanhassen, Minn.: The Child's World, 2001.

Web Sites

Visit our homepage for lots of links about *Brown v. Board of Education:*

http://www.childsworld.com/links.html

Note to Parents, Teachers, and Librarians:
We routinely verify our Web links to make sure they're safe,
active sites—so encourage your readers to check them out!

About the Author

Barbara A. Somervill is the author of several nonfiction books for young readers. She also writes video scripts and textbooks. She enjoys reading, painting, doing needlework, and playing bridge. She is a graduate of Saint Lawrence University in Canton, New York.